Fathering Strong
Fatherhood Workshop

Participant Workbook

BRUCE STAPLETON

Table of Contents

Welcome To Your Fatherhood Journey

Welcome to the Fathering Strong Workshop, a transformative 12-week journey to equip you with the spiritual foundation, practical tools, and supportive community needed to lead your family with purpose and confidence. Through biblical teaching, personal reflection, and actionable assignments, you will develop a comprehensive vision for your role as a father and create sustainable practices for lasting impact.

This workshop requires the book *"Fathering Strong - God's Blueprint for Leading Your Family"* by Bruce Stapleton to complete the program. Throughout the workshop, you may use the 30-Day Devotional and Journal that is referenced, or you may review and download the necessary resources at the website www.fatheringstrongbook.com.

This workbook serves as your personal guide. In these pages, you'll find space to record insights, complete exercises, track your progress, and document your growth as a father. Each week builds upon the previous one, creating a cohesive path toward stronger, more intentional fatherhood.

As you begin this journey, remember that becoming a stronger father isn't about perfection—it's about progress. It's about developing the courage to face challenges head-on, the fortitude to persist through difficulties, the faith to trust God's guidance, and the love that transforms everyday moments into lasting memories.

Whether you're a new father seeking to start strong, a seasoned dad looking to refine your approach, or somewhere in between, this workshop offers valuable insights and practical strategies to help you become the father God designed you to be.

Let's embark on this journey together, supporting one another as we grow in our most important calling—fathering strong.

How To Use This Workbook

This workbook is designed to maximize your growth throughout the 12-week Fathering Strong Workshop. To get the most from this experience follow these guidelines.

> ➤ **Before Each Session:** Complete the reading assigned in the previous section and review the reflection questions for the upcoming week. Come prepared to engage fully with the material and your fellow fathers.

> ➤ **During Each Session:** Use the note-taking space to record key insights, questions, and action steps. Active participation enhances your learning and contributes to the group's growth.

> ➤ **After Each Session:** Implement the weekly assignments, reflecting on how the principles apply to your unique family situation. The real transformation happens between our meetings as you put these concepts into practice.

> ➤ **Throughout the Week:** Refer back to your notes and commitments. Consider setting aside specific times for reflection and implementation. Share your learning with your spouse or a trusted friend for additional accountability.

> ➤ **For Ongoing Growth:** The final section of this workbook reviews resources for continued development beyond our 12 weeks together. Your fatherhood journey doesn't end with this workshop—it's just beginning.

Remember, this workbook is a personal tool for your growth. Be honest in your reflections, specific in your goals, and diligent in your follow-through. The effort you invest in here will yield dividends in your family for generations to come.

Workshop Overview

The 12-week journey is carefully structured to build a comprehensive foundation for strong fatherhood. Each session follows a consistent format:

Session Format (60 minutes)

> ➤ Welcome & Check-in (5 minutes)

> ➤ Review of Previous Week's Assignment (10 minutes)

> ➤ Core Teaching & Discussion (30 minutes)

> ➤ Small Group Application Exercise (10 minutes)

> ➤ Next Steps & Assignment Overview (5 minutes)

Weekly Topics:

Week 1: The Call to Fathering Strong

Week 2: God as Father – Our Perfect Model

Week 3: Courage and Fortitude – Facing Fatherhood Head On

Week 4: Faith and Love – The Anchoring Core Virtues of a Fathering Strong Life

Week 5: Physical Health – Fueling Your Body and Mind

Week 6: Spiritual Health – Connecting with the True Father

Week 7: Emotional Wealth – Mastering Your Inner World

Week 8: Financial Wisdom – Stewarding God's Resources as a Father

Week 9: A Strong Marriage – The Foundation of the Family

Week 10: Building Lasting Bonds with Your Children

Week 11: Setting Your Goals and Putting it all Together

Week 12: Building Your Legacy and Starting the 30-Day Devotional and Journal

You'll develop practical skills in these areas throughout our time together while building meaningful connections with other fathers. By the end of the 12 weeks, you'll have a comprehensive blueprint for leading your family with purpose, confidence, and biblical wisdom.

My Fathering Strong Commitment

As I begin this 12-week journey, I make the following commitments to myself, my family, and my fellow participants:

➢ I will attend each session, arriving prepared and on time.

➢ I will engage honestly in discussions, sharing both my struggles and victories.

➢ I will complete the weekly readings and assignments to the best of my ability.

➢ I will set meaningful goals each week and work diligently to achieve them.

➢ I will meet regularly with my accountability partner, being both honest about my challenges and encouraging about his.

➢ I will apply what I learn to my daily life, seeking to grow as a father each week.

➢ I will pray for the other men in this workshop and support them on their journeys.

➢ I understand that my growth as a father will directly impact my family, and I commit to this process for their benefit and God's glory.

Signature: _____

Date: _____

Accountability Partner or Workshop Facilitator: _____

Week 1: The Call to Fathering Strong

Session Overview

In this first session, we'll explore God's divine calling for fathers and introduce the four pillars of Fathering Strong: courage, fortitude, faith, and love. You'll begin crafting your personal fatherhood vision and connect with other fathers on the same journey. By the end of this session, you'll understand fatherhood as a sacred calling rather than just a role and have clarity about the kind of father God designed you to be.

Scripture Focus: "Be on your guard; stand firm in the faith; be courageous; be strong. Do everything in love." (1 Corinthians 16:13-14)

Reflection Questions

Where are you currently in your fatherhood journey?

What aspects of fathering do you feel confident about, and where do you desire growth?

What does it mean to you to be "Fathering Strong"?

How might this differ from cultural definitions of successful fatherhood?

Think about your own father or father figures in your life. What positive qualities would you like to emulate?

What aspects would you like to do differently?

Session Notes

Key Insights from today's session:

> ➢ Understanding fatherhood as a divine calling rather than just a role

> ➢ The four pillars of Fathering Strong: courage, fortitude, faith, and love

> ➢ How these virtues work together to build a strong foundation for your family

> ➢ The difference between success-focused and significance-focused fatherhood

Questions I want to explore further:

SMALL GROUP DISCUSSION

Share your current fatherhood journey: Where are you now? What brought you to this workshop?

Discuss your vision for fatherhood: What kind of father do you aspire to be? What legacy do you hope to leave?

Notes from group discussion:

This Week's Assignment

Reading:
Fathering Strong – God's Blueprint for Leading Your Family: Introduction and Chapters 1 and 2 *Fathering Strong – 30-Day Devotional and Journal*: Introduction and Complete Day 1 of the 7-Day Awakening – Fatherhood Vision

Action Steps: Begin crafting your personal fatherhood vision statement using the provided template.

My Personal Commitment: This week, I will take the following specific steps toward becoming a stronger father:

Prayer Focus for the Week: Lord, help me to understand Your vision for my role as a father. Open my heart to grow in the areas where I need development. Give me clarity about the kind of father You've designed me to be and the courage to pursue that calling with my whole heart. Amen.

--Notes--

Week 2: God As Father – Our Perfect Model

Session Overview

In this session, we'll explore God's perfect model of fatherhood and how we can reflect His character in our parenting. You'll discover God's four essential roles as Father and develop practical ways to embody these qualities in your daily interactions with your children. By the end of this session, you'll have a deeper understanding of how viewing God as the perfect father reshapes your approach to fatherhood.

Scripture Focus: *"As a father has compassion on his children, so the LORD has compassion on those who fear him."* (Psalm 103:13)

Reflection Questions

How does understanding God as your Heavenly Father impact your approach to fathering your children?

In what ways do you see God functioning as Protector, Order Keeper, Provider, and Stabilizer in your life? How might you reflect these qualities in your fatherhood?

What aspects of God's fatherhood do you find most challenging to emulate? Why?

Session Notes

Key Insights from Today's Teaching:

➢ The four essential roles God models as Father: Protector, Order Keeper, Provider, and Stabilizer

➢ How viewing God as the perfect father reshapes our understanding of our own role

➢ Practical ways to reflect God's character in your daily interactions with your children

➢ The significance of "The Armor of God" as our shield and protection in fatherhood

➢ Building a spiritual foundation that guides your family through life's challenges

Questions I want to explore further:

Small Group Discussion

Share about your relationship with God as Father: How has your understanding of God as Father been shaped by your experiences? How is it evolving?

Discuss one aspect of God's fatherhood you want to develop in your own parenting: What practical steps might help you grow in this area?

Notes from group discussion:

This Week's Assignment

Reading:

Fathering Strong – God's Blueprint for Leading Your Family: Chapters 3 and 4

Action Steps: Continue developing your fatherhood vision based on biblical principles. Identify one area where you can better reflect God's fatherhood in your family this week.

My Personal Commitment: This week, I will take the following specific steps toward becoming a stronger father:

Prayer Focus for the Week: Heavenly Father, thank You for being my perfect example of fatherhood. Help me to understand more deeply how You father me so I can better reflect Your character to my children. This week, show me specific ways to demonstrate Your protection, order, provision, and stability in my home. Amen.

--Notes--

Week 3: Courage And Fortitude – Facing Fatherhood Head On

Session Overview

In this session, we'll explore the essential virtues of courage and fortitude that enable fathers to face challenges head-on. You'll learn practical strategies for making difficult decisions, having tough conversations, and persisting through parenting obstacles. By the end of this session, you'll understand how developing these strengths can transform your approach to fatherhood and equip you to lead your family with confidence, even in uncertain times.

Scripture Focus: "Have I not commanded you? Be strong and courageous. Do not be afraid; do not be discouraged, for the LORD your God will be with you wherever you go." (Joshua 1:9)

Reflection Questions

What situations in your fatherhood journey currently require the most courage? What makes these situations challenging?

How would you define fortitude in the context of fatherhood? When have you demonstrated this quality?

In what ways might fear be holding you back from being the father God has called you to be?

Session Notes

Key Insights from today's session:

> ➤ How courage enables you to make difficult decisions, have tough conversations, and stand firm in your values:

> ➤ Real-life examples of everyday courage in fatherhood (setting boundaries, admitting mistakes, facing the unknown):

> ➤ Cultivating fortitude – the unwavering strength to persist through challenges and setbacks:

> ➤ Practical strategies for developing resilience in both yourself and your children:

> ➤ The connection between courage, vulnerability, and authentic leadership:

Questions I want to explore further:

Small Group Discussion

Share about a time when fatherhood required courage: What was the situation? How did you respond? What did you learn?

Discuss areas where you need to develop more fortitude: What specific challenges require persistent strength in your fatherhood journey?

Notes from group discussion:

This Week's Assignment

Reading:

Fathering Strong – God's Blueprint for Leading Your Family: Chapters 5 and 6

Fathering Strong – 30-Day Devotional and Journal: Complete Day 2 of the 7-Day Awakening – Fatherhood Assessment

Action Steps: Identify one situation requiring courage you're currently facing as a father and develop an action plan.

My Personal Commitment: This week, I will take the following specific steps toward becoming a stronger father:

Prayer Focus for the Week: Lord, grant me the courage to face the challenges of fatherhood head-on. Help me develop the fortitude to persist when parenting gets difficult. Show me where fear might be holding me back, and give me the strength to confidently move forward, knowing You are with me. Amen.

--Notes--

Week 4: Faith And Love – The Anchoring Core Virtues of a Fathering Strong Life

Session Overview

In this session, we'll explore how faith and love serve as two of the four core virtues for effective fatherhood. You'll discover practical ways to integrate faith into your parenting decisions and learn how to demonstrate love as an action rather than just an emotion. By the end of this session, you'll understand how these two virtues work together to transform challenging parenting situations and create a lasting legacy for your family.

Scripture Focus: "And now these three remain: faith, hope, and love. But the greatest of these is love." (1 Corinthians 13:13)

Reflection Questions

How does your faith influence your approach to fatherhood? In what ways does it provide guidance and strength?

What does it mean to you to father with love? How do you express love to your children in ways that are meaningful to them?

How might growing in faith and love transform your most challenging parenting situations?

Session Notes

Key Insights from today's session:

➢ Building a living faith that guides your decisions and actions as a father:

➢ How faith in God's promises provides stability during family challenges:

➢ Understanding love as an action rather than just an emotion:

➢ Practical ways to demonstrate unconditional love while maintaining healthy boundaries:

➢ Creating a legacy of faith and love that impacts future generations:

Questions I want to explore further:

Small Group Discussion

Share about how faith influences your fatherhood: In what ways does your relationship with God shape how you parent?

Discuss how you express love to your children: What have you found most effective? What would you like to improve?

Notes from group discussion:

This Week's Assignment

Reading: *Fathering Strong – God's Blueprint for Leading Your Family:* Part 2 and Chapters 7 and 8

Action Steps: Begin identifying specific SMART goals for strengthening your fatherhood journey. Practice one new way to demonstrate love to each family member this week.

My Personal Commitment: This week, I will take the following specific steps toward becoming a stronger father:

Prayer Focus for the Week: Heavenly Father, deepen my faith so I can lead my family with confidence and wisdom. Teach me to love as You love—unconditionally, sacrificially, and consistently. Help me demonstrate faith and love in practical ways that my children can understand and embrace. Amen.

--Notes--

Week 5: Physical Health – Fueling Your Body and Mind

Session Overview

In this session, we'll explore how physical health serves as a foundation for effective fatherhood. You'll learn practical strategies for developing sustainable fitness habits, creating nutritional plans, and implementing stress management techniques that work within a busy father's schedule. By the end of this session, you'll understand how caring for your body directly impacts your energy, patience, and capacity to lead your family well.

Scripture Focus: "Do you not know that your bodies are temples of the Holy Spirit, who is in you, whom you have received from God? You are not your own; you were bought at a price. Therefore, honor God with your bodies." (1 Corinthians 6:19-20)

Reflection Questions

How would you rate your current physical health?

What impact does your physical condition have on your effectiveness as a father?

What are your biggest challenges when it comes to maintaining physical health (exercise, nutrition, sleep, stress management)?

How might improving your physical health positively affect your family relationships?

Session Notes

Key Insights from today's session:

> The Lifegevity approach to balanced physical health (exercise, nutrition, relaxation):

> Developing sustainable fitness habits that work within a busy father's schedule:

> Creating nutritional strategies that fuel your body and set an example for your family:

> Practical relaxation techniques to manage stress and maintain emotional balance:

> Setting SMART goals for physical health that support your fatherhood vision:

Questions I want to explore further:

Small Group Discussion

Share about your current physical health habits: What's working well? What would you like to improve?

Discuss the connection between physical health and fatherhood: How does your physical condition affect your energy, patience, and engagement with your children?

Notes from group discussion:

This Week's Assignment

Reading: *Fathering Strong – God's Blueprint for Leading Your Family:* Chapter 9

Fathering Strong – 30-Day Devotional and Journal: Complete Day 3 of the 7-Day Awakening

Action Steps: Develop 2-3 SMART goals for improving your physical health to support your fatherhood.

My Personal Commitment: This week, I will take the following specific steps toward becoming a stronger father:

Prayer Focus for the Week: Lord, help me to honor You by caring for the body You've given me. Show me how to develop sustainable habits of exercise, nutrition, and rest that will fuel my fatherhood journey. Give me the wisdom to make choices that increase my energy and capacity to serve my family well. Amen.

--Notes--

Week 6: Spiritual Health – Connecting with the True Father

Session Overview

This session will explore how spiritual health forms the foundation of effective fatherhood. You'll learn practical strategies for deepening your relationship with God through prayer, Bible study, and community. By the end of this session, you'll understand how your spiritual vitality directly impacts your ability to lead your family with wisdom and purpose, and you'll have concrete tools for growing as a spiritual leader in your home.

Scripture Focus: "But grow in the grace and knowledge of our Lord and Savior Jesus Christ." (2 Peter 3:18)

Reflection Questions

How would you describe your current spiritual health? What practices help you connect with God?

In what ways does your spiritual life influence your approach to fatherhood?

What spiritual disciplines would you like to develop or strengthen to become a better spiritual leader for your family?

Session Notes

Key Insights from today's session:

➢ Establishing consistent prayer practices that strengthen your relationship with God

➢ Developing Bible study habits that provide wisdom for family leadership

➢ Building community with other fathers for support, accountability, and growth

➢ Practical ways to live out your faith through service and compassion

➢ Leading your family in spiritual development through both teaching and example

Questions I want to explore further:

Small Group Discussion

Share about your spiritual journey: What has been most formative in your relationship with God? How has this shaped your fatherhood?

Discuss challenges to spiritual leadership in your home: What obstacles do you face? What strategies have been helpful?

Notes from group discussion:

This Week's Assignment

Reading: *Fathering Strong – God's Blueprint for Leading Your Family:* Chapter 10

Action Steps: Begin implementing a daily spiritual practice from the chapter. Identify one way to increase your family's spiritual connection this week.

My Personal Commitment: This week, I will take the following specific steps toward becoming a stronger father:

Prayer Focus for the Week: Heavenly Father, draw me closer to You so I can better reflect Your character to my children. Help me establish consistent spiritual practices that nurture my relationship with You. Show me how to lead my family spiritually in ways that are authentic and meaningful. Amen.

--Notes--

Week 7: Emotional Wealth – Mastering Your Inner World

Session Overview

This session will explore how emotional intelligence impacts your effectiveness as a father. You'll learn practical strategies for managing emotions, responding thoughtfully to challenges, and creating an emotionally safe environment for your family. By the end of this session, you'll understand how your emotional wealth directly influences your relationships and have concrete tools for developing greater self-awareness and emotional regulation.

Scripture Focus: "Above all else, guard your heart, for everything you do flows from it." (Proverbs 4:23)

Reflection Questions

How would you describe your emotional health? What are your strengths and growth areas?

How do your emotions affect your parenting? Can you identify patterns or triggers?

What tools or practices help you manage difficult emotions effectively?

Session Notes

Key Insights from today's session:

> ➤ Developing emotional regulation skills to respond rather than react
>
> ➤ Effective stress management techniques designed explicitly for fathers
>
> ➤ The power of vulnerability in building authentic relationships with your children
>
> ➤ Communication strategies that foster understanding and connection
>
> ➤ Creating an emotionally safe environment where your family can thrive

Questions I want to explore further:

Small Group Discussion

Share about your emotional journey as a father: What emotions do you find most challenging? What has helped you grow emotionally?

Discuss the impact of emotional health on your family: How does your emotional state affect your children and spouse?

Notes from group discussion:

This Week's Assignment

Reading: *Fathering Strong – God's Blueprint for Leading Your Family:* Chapter 11

Fathering Strong – 30-Day Devotional and Journal: Complete Day 4 of the 7-Day Awakening

Action Steps: Identify your emotional triggers and develop a specific plan for managing them.

My Personal Commitment: This week, I will take the following specific steps toward becoming a stronger father:

Prayer Focus for the Week: Lord, help me develop greater emotional intelligence and self-awareness. Teach me to manage my emotions in ways that create safety and connection for my family. Give me the courage to be vulnerable with my children and the wisdom to create an emotionally healthy home. Amen.

--Notes--

Week 8: Financial Wisdom – Stewarding God's Resources as a Father

Session Overview

This session will explore biblical financial stewardship and its impact on effective fatherhood. You'll learn practical strategies for budgeting, saving, investing, and teaching financial principles to your children. By the end of this session, you'll understand how sound financial management creates security for your family and demonstrates godly values through your example.

Scripture Focus: "Honor the LORD with your wealth, with the first fruits of all your crops." (Proverbs 3:9)

Reflection Questions

How would you describe your current approach to financial management? What principles guide your decisions?

How does your financial stewardship impact your family's well-being and security?

What financial habits or skills would you like to develop or improve?

Session Notes

Key Insights from today's session:

➤ Creating a God-centered budget that aligns with your family's values

➤ Saving and investing strategies to secure your family's future

➤ Biblical principles of stewardship and generosity

➤ Breaking free from debt and financial bondage

➤ Teaching your children sound financial principles through both instruction and example

Questions I want to explore further:

Small Group Discussion

Share about your financial journey: What challenges have you faced? What victories have you experienced?

Discuss how you approach financial teaching with your children: What methods have been effective? What would you like to improve?

Notes from group discussion:

This Week's Assignment

Reading: *Fathering Strong – God's Blueprint for Leading Your Family:* Chapter 12

Action Steps: Begin implementing one financial management tool discussed in the chapter. Create a specific plan for teaching one financial principle to your children this month.

My Personal Commitment: This week, I will take the following specific steps toward becoming a stronger father:

Prayer Focus for the Week: Heavenly Father, give me wisdom to manage the resources You've entrusted me. Help me create financial stability for my family while modeling generosity and wise stewardship. Show me how to teach my children biblical financial principles that will serve them throughout their lives. Amen.

--Notes--

Week 9: A Strong Marriage – The Foundation of the Family

Session Overview

This session will explore how a healthy marriage creates the foundation for effective family leadership. You'll learn practical strategies for strengthening your marital relationship through better communication, deeper intimacy, and shared values. By the end of this session, you'll understand how investing in your marriage directly enhances your effectiveness as a father and creates security for your children.

Scripture Focus: "Husbands, love your wives, just as Christ loved the church and gave himself up for her." (Ephesians 5:25)

Reflection Questions

How would you describe the current state of your marriage? What strengths and growth areas do you see?

In what ways does your marriage relationship impact your effectiveness as a father?

What specific actions help strengthen your connection with your spouse?

Session Notes

Key Insights from today's session:

➢ Biblical foundations for marriage and their impact on effective parenting

➢ Communication practices that strengthen your marital bond

➢ Developing deeper intimacy through physical, emotional, spiritual, and mental connection

➢ Aligning your values and priorities as a couple to create family unity

➢ Practical ways to demonstrate love, appreciation, and affection in your marriage

Questions I want to explore further:

Small Group Discussion

Share about the connection between your marriage and fatherhood: How does one influence the other?

Discuss strategies for strengthening your marriage: What practices have been most effective?

What would you like to improve?

Notes from group discussion:

This Week's Assignment

Reading: *Fathering Strong – God's Blueprint for Leading Your Family:* Chapter 13

Fathering Strong – 30-Day Devotional and Journal: Complete Day 5 of the 7-Day Awakening

Action Steps: Schedule a dedicated time with your spouse to discuss your shared family vision. Implement one new practice to strengthen your marriage this week.

My Personal Commitment: This week, I will take the following specific steps toward becoming **a stronger father:**

Prayer Focus for the Week: Lord, strengthen my marriage as the foundation of our family. Help me to love my spouse as Christ loves the church—sacrificially and unconditionally. This week, show me specific ways to build unity, deepen communication, and demonstrate appreciation. Amen.

--Notes--

Week 10: Building Lasting Bonds with Your Children

Session Overview

This session will explore strategies for developing meaningful connections with your children that stand the test of time. You'll learn age-appropriate approaches for understanding your children's unique needs, communicating effectively, and creating intentional moments that strengthen your relationship. By the end of this session, you'll have practical tools for building trust, demonstrating love, and guiding your children's development in ways that honor their individuality while instilling core values.

Scripture Focus: "Start children off on the way they should go, and even when they are old, they will not turn from it." (Proverbs 22:6)

Reflection Questions

How would you describe your current relationship with each of your children? What strengths and growth areas do you see?

What activities or practices help you connect meaningfully with your children?

How do you adapt your parenting approach to each child's unique personality and needs?

Session Notes

Key Insights from today's session:

> ➤ Understanding children's needs at different developmental stages
> ➤ The vital role of fathers in their children's identity formation
> ➤ Teaching core values through daily interactions and intentional conversations
> ➤ Effective communication strategies tailored to your child's age and personality
> ➤ Creating discipleship rhythms that strengthen your bond while guiding their growth

Questions I want to explore further:

Small Group Discussion

Share about your relationship with your children: What brings you joy? What challenges do you face?

Discuss strategies for connecting with each child individually: How do you make each child feel valued and understood?

Notes from group discussion:

This Week's Assignment

Reading: *Fathering Strong – God's Blueprint for Leading Your Family:* Part 3 and Chapters 14 & 15
Fathering Strong – 30-Day Devotional and Journal: Complete Day 6 of the 7-Day Awakening

Action Steps: Plan one meaningful connection activity with each child based on their unique interests. Begin implementing one new communication practice with your children.

My Personal Commitment: This week, I will take the following specific steps toward becoming a stronger father:

Prayer Focus for the Week: Heavenly Father, help me build lasting bonds with each of my children. Give me the wisdom to understand their unique needs and personalities. Show me how to communicate in ways that reach their hearts and guide their growth. Help me create meaningful moments that strengthen our connection. Amen.

--Notes--

Week 11: Setting Your Goals and Putting It All Together

Session Overview

In this session, we'll synthesize everything we've learned throughout the workshop into a cohesive fatherhood strategy. You'll develop specific, measurable goals across all six core strength areas and create a practical implementation plan. By the end of this session, you'll have a clear roadmap for continued growth as a father and concrete tools for tracking your progress and maintaining momentum.

Scripture Focus: "But as for me and my household, we will serve the LORD." (Joshua 24:15)

Reflection Questions

Looking back over the past 10 weeks, what key insights or principles have been most meaningful to you?

What specific areas of fatherhood do you feel called to strengthen or develop?

How might you integrate what you've learned into a cohesive approach to leading your family?

Session Notes

Key Insights from today's session:

> ➤ Reviewing the six core strengths of Fathering Strong and how they work together
> ➤ Creating SMART goals across each area that support your overall vision
> ➤ Developing practical tools for tracking progress and maintaining momentum
> ➤ Establishing accountability systems for lasting change
> ➤ Building a sustainable rhythm of reflection and adjustment

Questions I want to explore further:

Small Group Discussion

Share your key takeaways from the workshop: What has been most impactful?

How has your perspective on fatherhood changed?

Discuss your priority goals moving forward: What specific areas will you focus on first?

How will you measure progress?

Notes from group discussion:

This Week's Assignment

Reading: *Fathering Strong – God's Blueprint for Leading Your Family:* Chapters 16 & 17

Fathering Strong – 30-Day Devotional and Journal: Complete Day 7 of the 7-Day Awakening

Action Steps: Finalize your top 5 SMART goals using the prioritization framework. Identify an accountability partner for your fatherhood journey.

My Personal Commitment: This week, I will take the following specific steps toward becoming a stronger father:

Prayer Focus for the Week: Lord, help me integrate all I've learned into a cohesive vision for leading my family. Give me clarity about which areas to prioritize and wisdom to set meaningful goals. Show me how to build sustainable practices that will strengthen my fatherhood for years to come. Amen.

--Notes--

Week 12: Building Your Legacy and Starting The 30-Day Devotional and Journal

Session Overview

In this final session, we'll focus on creating a lasting legacy for your family and launching your ongoing growth journey. You'll learn how to transform your fatherhood vision into daily actions shaping future generations. By the end of this session, you'll clearly understand legacy building beyond material inheritance and a structured plan to continue your development through the 30-Day Devotional and Journal.

Scripture Focus: "A good person leaves an inheritance for their children's children, but a sinner's wealth is stored up for the righteous." (Proverbs 13:22)

Reflection Questions

What legacy do you want to leave for your children and future generations?

How does this shape your approach to fatherhood?

How will you maintain momentum in your fatherhood journey after this workshop ends?

What support systems will help you continue growing as a father?

Session Notes

Key Insights from today's session:

➤ Understanding legacy as more than material inheritance

➤ How your daily choices shape your family for generations

➤ Creating traditions that reflect your values and strengthen family bonds

➤ Developing a sustainable plan for ongoing growth beyond the workshop

➤ Launching your 30-day devotional journey with purpose and commitment

Questions I want to explore further:

Small Group Discussion

Share about the legacy you want to create: What values, traditions, and memories do you want to pass on?

Discuss your plan for continued growth: How will you maintain momentum after the workshop ends?

Notes from group discussion:

This Week's Assignment

Reading:

Fathering Strong – 30-Day Devotional and Journal: Read Part 2 and chapters on Transforming Vision into Action and Your Legacy Begins Today

Action Steps: Begin your 30-Day Devotional practice using the tools provided. Schedule regular check-ins with your accountability partner. Create a celebration plan to mark your progress at 30, 60, and 90 days.

My Personal Commitment: Moving forward, I will take the following specific steps toward becoming a stronger father:

Prayer Focus for the Week: Heavenly Father, thank You for guiding me through this fatherhood journey. Help me build a legacy that honors You and blesses my family for generations. Give me perseverance to continue growing as a father, wisdom to implement what I've learned, and joy in the journey ahead. Amen.

--Notes--

Continuing Your Journey: Resources For Ongoing Growth

Fathering Strong Community

The journey of fatherhood wasn't meant to be walked alone. Connect with other fathers through:

- ➤ **The Fathering Strong App:** Access resources, join discussion forums, and find local events.

- ➤ **Local Fathering Strong Groups:** Continue meeting with fathers in your area for ongoing support and accountability.

- ➤ **Online Communities:** Participate in virtual gatherings and webinars for continued learning.

Recommended Reading

- ➤ **Father Love – The Powerful Resource Every Child Needs,** by Pastor Eli Williams

- ➤ **Point Man,** by Steve Farrar

- ➤ **Wild at Heart,** by John Eldredge

- ➤ **Strong Fathers, Strong Daughters,** by Meg Meeker

Additional Resources

Fathering Strong Website: (WWW.FATHERINGSTRONG.COM): Articles, videos, and downloadable tools for continued growth.

Fathering Strong Podcast: Weekly episodes featuring interviews, teaching, and practical fatherhood strategies found on YouTube, Spotify and Apple podcasts.

Annual Fathering Strong Conference: Join hundreds of fathers for intensive training and encouragement.

MY ONGOING GROWTH PLAN

Regular Practices I Will Maintain:

Accountability Structure:

Resources I Will Utilize:

How I Will Measure Progress:

My Vision for the Next Year of Fatherhood:

Appendix A: Smart Goal Framework

Understanding Smart Goals

SMART goals transform vague intentions into clear, actionable plans. Each letter in the **SMART** acronym represents a critical component:

> ➢ **Specific**: Clearly define what you want to accomplish. Instead of "spend more time with my kids," try "have one-on-one time with each child for 30 minutes twice weekly."

> ➢ **Measurable:** Include concrete criteria to track progress. "Read to my children for 15 minutes each night" is measurable; "Read more to my children" is not.

> ➢ **Achievable:** Set realistic goals within your current life context. Consider your schedule, resources, and other commitments.

> ➢ **Relevant:** Align goals with your fatherhood priorities and values. Each goal should connect directly to your vision statement.

> ➢ **Time-bound:** Establish clear deadlines and milestones. "Start family devotions by next Monday" creates an urgency that "start family devotions someday" lacks.

Smart Goal Examples For Each Core Strength Area

Physical health: "I will exercise for 30 minutes three times per week for the next month, scheduling these sessions on Monday, Wednesday, and Friday mornings."

Spiritual health: "I will read one chapter from Proverbs each morning for the next 31 days, journaling at least one insight about fatherhood from each reading."

Emotional Wealth: "I will practice the 'pause and pray' technique before responding when frustrated with my children, tracking my success rate daily for the next two weeks."

Financial wisdom: "I will create a family budget by the end of this month and review it weekly with my spouse for the following three months."

Marriage Relationship: "I will schedule a weekly 30-minute check-in conversation with my spouse every Sunday evening for the next two months, using the provided conversation starters."

Child Connections: "I will have individual 'dad dates' with each of my children once per month for the next six months, letting them choose the activity within our budget parameters."

SMART Goal Worksheet

Use this template to develop your own SMART goals for each core strength area:

Core Strength Area:

My SMART Goal:

Specific: What exactly will I accomplish?

Measurable: How will I track progress?

Achievable: Is this realistic with my current resources?

Relevant: How does this connect to my vision?

Time-bound: When will I accomplish this?

Why this matters to me and my family:

Potential obstacles and solutions:

First action step:

How I'll celebrate achieving this goal:

A Father's Prayer

Heavenly Father,

As we conclude this journey of growth and transformation, we come before You with grateful hearts. Thank You for calling us to the sacred responsibility of fatherhood and for equipping us through Your Word and this fellowship of fathers.

Lord, we acknowledge that we cannot be Fathering Strong without Your strength. Pour out Your wisdom upon us as we return to our homes and families. May the seeds planted during these twelve weeks take deep root in our hearts and bear fruit in our daily lives.

Grant us the courage to face the challenges of fatherhood head-on, fortitude to persist when the path grows difficult, faith to trust Your guidance when we cannot see the way forward, and love that reflects Your perfect love for us.

Help us steward our physical bodies with discipline, nurture our spiritual lives with devotion, manage our emotions with wisdom, handle our finances with integrity, cherish our marriages with tenderness, and build lasting bonds with our children through intentional presence.

When we falter, remind us that Your grace is sufficient. When we succeed, let us give You the glory. In moments of uncertainty, bring to mind the principles and practices we've learned together.

Lord, we ask for Your blessing upon our families. May our children grow strong in body, mind, and spirit under our care. May they see in us a reflection of Your fatherhood and be drawn to You through our example.

Strengthen the brotherhood we've formed here. Help us continue to support, encourage, and hold one another accountable as we strive to father according to Your design.

Finally, Father, we commit to building legacies that honor You. May the impact of our fatherhood extend far beyond our lifetimes, influencing generations we will never meet. May our children's children rise up and call You blessed because of the foundation we lay today.

We pray this with humble hearts, recognizing our dependence on You, the perfect Father from whom all fatherhood derives its name.

In the name of Jesus Christ, our Lord and Savior,

Amen.

For more resources go to:

www.fatheringstrongbook.com

Purchase the book that accompanies this workshop

Fathering Strong – God's Blueprint for Leading Your Family

Purchase online at all major book outlets.

12-week Workshop for Churches

Interested in starting a fatherhood class? Participant Workbooks and Facilitator Guides are available with the book and other resources. Certificates are available for participants. Contact information@fatheringstrongbook.com for bundle discounts.

Join a fatherhood community where you can connect with other fathers, get support and encouragement throughout your fatherhood journey, and become empowered to be the best dad you can be. Join this free community today!

Join at www.fatheringstrong.com